HOLIDAY JOKES

Compiled by Pam Rosenberg • Illustrated by Mernie Gallagher-Cole

Published by The Child's World®
1980 Lookout Drive
Mankato, MN 56003-1705
800-599-READ
www.childsworld.com

The Child's World®: Mary Berendes, Publishing Director
Editorial Directions, Inc.: E. Russell Primm, Editorial
Director; Lucia Raatma, Copyeditor and Proofreader;
Jennifer Zeiger and Joshua Gregory, Editorial Assistants
The Design Lab: Design and production

Library of Congress Cataloging-in-Publication Data
Holiday jokes / compiled by Pam Rosenberg ;
illustrated by Mernie Gallagher-Cole.
    p. cm.
  ISBN 978-1-60253-519-0 (library bound : alk. paper)
  1. Holidays—Juvenile humor. I. Rosenberg, Pam.
II. Gallagher-Cole, Mernie. III. Title.
  PN6231.H547H66 2010
  818'.602080334—dc22   2010002050

Printed in the United States of America
Mankato, Minnesota
December 2010
PA02082

ABOUT THE AUTHOR

Pam Rosenberg is the author of more than 50 books for children. She lives near Chicago, Illinois, with her husband and two children.

ABOUT THE ILLUSTRATOR

Mernie Gallagher-Cole lives in Pennsylvania with her husband and two children. She has illustrated many books for The Child's World®.

TABLE OF CONTENTS

4 Valentine's Day

6 Saint Patrick's Day

7 Easter

10 A Mother's Day Joke

10 A Father's Day Joke

11 Fourth of July (Independence Day)

14 Halloween

18 Thanksgiving

21 Christmas

24 Birthday Jokes

VALENTINE'S DAY

KNOCK, KNOCK.
Who's there?
Oscar.
    Oscar who?
    Oscar if she likes me!

Q: What do you call two birds in love?
A: Tweet-hearts.

....

Q: What did the man with the broken leg say
to his nurse?
A: "I've got a crutch on you."

....

Q: What do you call a very small valentine?
A: A valen-tiny.

....

Q: Did you hear about the nearsighted porcupine?
A: He fell in love with a pincushion.

Q: Did you hear about the romance in the tropical fish tank?

A: It was a case of guppy love.

....

Q: What did one calculator say to the other calculator?

A: "How do I love thee? Let me count the ways!"

....

Q: What did the paper clip say to the magnet?

A: "I find you very attractive."

....

Q: What did the boy octopus say to the girl octopus on Valentine's Day?

A: "I want to hold your hand, hand, hand, hand, hand, hand, hand, hand."

....

Q: What do squirrels get on Valentine's Day?

A: Forget-me-nuts.

....

Q: Do skunks celebrate Valentine's Day?

A: Of course! They're very scent-imental.

SAINT PATRICK'S DAY

TEACHER: Why did St. Patrick drive the snakes out of Ireland?
STUDENT: Because it was too far for them to crawl.

Q: What did one Irish ghost say to the other?
A: "Top o' the moaning!"

Q: Why can't you borrow money from leprechauns?
A: Because they're always a little short.

Q: Why should you never iron a four-leaf clover?
A: Because you never want to press your luck.

Q: What do you get when two leprechauns have a conversation?
A: A lot of small talk.

Q: How do you catch the Easter Bunny?

A: Hide in the bushes and make a noise like a carrot.

....

Q: What is the Easter Bunny's favorite state capital?

A: Albunny, New York.

....

Q: Where does Dracula keep his Easter candy?

A: In his Easter casket.

....

Q: What's white and fluffy and rolls down a hill?

A: Peter Cottonball.

....

Q: Why did the Easter egg hide?

A: Because it was a little chicken.

....

Q: Did you hear about the lady whose house was infested with Easter eggs?

A: She had to call an eggs-terminator.

Q: Where does the Easter bunny get his eggs?

A: From an egg-plant.

....

Q: Why does Peter Cottontail hop down the bunny trail?

A: Because Mr. and Mrs. Cottontail won't let him borrow the car.

....

Q: How does the Easter Bunny stay healthy?

A: Eggs-ercise.

KNOCK, KNOCK.
Who's there?
Candy.
Candy who?
Candy Easter Bunny carry all those treats in one basket?

Q: What do you call the Easter Bunny on the day after Easter?

A: Tired.

....

Q: A man wanted an Easter pet for his daughter. He looked at a baby chick and a baby duck. They were both cute, but he decided to buy the baby chick. Do you know why?

A: The baby chick was a little cheeper!

....

Q: What has big ears, brings Easter treats, and goes "hippity-BOOM, hippity-BOOM, hippity-BOOM"?

A: The Easter Elephant.

....

Q: What do you call an Easter bunny from outer space?

A: An egg-straterrestrial.

....

Q: Why did the Easter Bunny have to fire the duck?

A: He kept quacking all the eggs.

A MOTHER'S DAY JOKE

Q: What does Frankenstein's monster do on Mother's Day?
A: He sends a dozen roses to the electric company.

A FATHER'S DAY JOKE

Q: Did you hear about the little boy who was named after his father?
A: His parents called him Dad.

FOURTH OF JULY
(INDEPENDENCE DAY)

TEACHER: True or False?
The Declaration of
Independence was
written in Philadelphia.

STUDENT: False. It was written in ink.

....

Q: Why did the British soldiers wear red coats?

A: So they could hide in the tomatoes.

....

Q: What did one flag say to the other flag?

A: Nothing. It just waved.

....

Q: What's red, white, blue, and ugly?

A: The Revolutionary Warthog.

....

Q: How was the food at the Fourth of
July picnic?

A: The hot dogs were bad, but the brats were
the wurst!

Q: Why did Paul Revere ride from Boston to Lexington?

A: Because the horse was too heavy to carry.

....

Q: What was General Washington's favorite tree?

A: The infantry.

....

Q: What's red, white, blue, and green?

A: A patriotic pickle.

....

Q: Why is the Liberty Bell like a dropped Easter egg?

A: They're both cracked.

....

Q: What is Uncle Sam's favorite snack?

A: Fire-crackers.

....

Q: Why did the duck say, "Bang"?

A: He was a fire-quacker.

....

Q: What happened as a result of the Stamp Act?

A: The Americans licked the British.

Q: What did King George think of the American colonists?

A: He thought they were revolting!

....

Q: How did American colonists' dogs protest against England?

A: The Boston Flea Party.

....

Q: What do you call an American revolutionary who draws cartoons?

A: Yankee Doodler.

HALLOWEEN

KNOCK, KNOCK.
Who's there?
Ivan.
Ivan who?
Ivan to bite your neck!

KNOCK, KNOCK.
Who's there?
Freighter.
Freighter who?
Freighter ghosts, are you?

KNOCK, KNOCK.
Who's there?
Ghost.
Ghost who?
Ghost to show you don't remember my name!

Q: What's orange on the inside and clear on the outside?

A: A pumpkin in a plastic bag.

....

Q: Did you hear about the ghost mortician?

A: He lived in a haunted hearse.

....

Q: What game do monster children play?

A: Hyde and shriek.

....

Q: What's nine feet tall and flies a kite in a rainstorm?

A: Benjamin Franklinstein.

....

Q: What evil crone turns off all the lamps on Halloween?

A: The light's witch.

....

Q: Why is a ghost like an empty house?

A: Because there's no body there.

Q: What do you call a dog owned by Dracula?
A: A bloodhound.

Q: What do you do with a green monster?
A: Put it in the sun until it ripens.

Q: Why did the vampire go to the blood bank?
A: He wanted to make a withdrawal.

Q: What did the vampire call his sweetheart?
A: His vein squeeze.

Q: Why is a graveyard so noisy?
A: Because of all the coffin.

Q: What is a witch's favorite subject in school?
A: Spelling.

Q: What happened when the vampire met the werewolf?
A: They became the best of fiends.

Q: What's a vampire's favorite cartoon character?
A: Batman.

Q: What happened when the ghost disappeared in the fog?
A: He was mist.

Q: Did you hear about the ghost who went on a safari?
A: He became a big game haunter.

Q: What do you call a person who lives next door to a vampire?
A: A tasty midnight snack.

Q: Why don't skeletons like to go to parties?
A: Because they have no body to dance with.

THANKSGIVING

KNOCK, KNOCK.
Who's there?
Arthur.
Arthur who?
Arthur any leftovers?

Q: Who's never hungry on Thanksgiving?
A; The turkey. He's always stuffed.

Q: What kind of key has two legs and can't open doors?
A: A tur-key.

SHEILA: I was going to serve sweet potatoes with Thanksgiving dinner, but I sat on them.
TOM: What are you serving instead?
SHEILA: Squash.

Q: Why was the monster tickled when he ate the turkey?

A: He forgot to pluck the feathers.

. . . .

Q: What do you get if you cross a turkey with an evil spirit?

A: A poultry-geist.

. . . .

Q: What do you get after eating way too much turkey and dressing?

A: Dessert.

. . . .

Q: Why shouldn't you look at the turkey dressing?

A: It makes her blush.

. . . .

Q: If April showers bring May flowers, what do May flowers bring?

A: Pilgrims.

. . . .

TEACHER: What are you thankful for this Thanksgiving?

STUDENT: I'm thankful I'm not a turkey.

Q: When did the Pilgrims first say "God bless America"?

A: The first time they heard America sneeze.

....

Q: Why did the turkey cross the road?

A: It was the chicken's day off.

....

Q: Why should you never talk like a turkey?

A: Because it's bad to use fowl language.

....

Q: What sound does a space turkey make?

A: "Hubble, hubble, hubble."

....

Q: What is a pilgrim's favorite kind of music?

A: Plymouth Rock.

....

Q: What did the turkey say to the turkey hunter?

A: "Quack, quack, quack."

....

Q: What's the best way to stuff a turkey?

A: Take him out for pizza and ice cream.

KNOCK, KNOCK.
Who's there?
Murray.
Murray who?
Murray Christmas to all,
and to all a good night!

CHRISTMAS

KNOCK, KNOCK.
Who's there?
Avery
Avery who?
Avery merry Christmas
to you!

....

KNOCK, KNOCK.
Who's there?
Dexter.
Dexter who?
Dexter halls with boughs of holly.

Q: Why did the reindeer wear sunglasses to the beach?
A: He didn't want to be recognized.

Q: What do you get when Santa Claus goes down a chimney and the fire is lit?
A: Crisp Kringle.

....

Q: What do you give a mummy for Christmas?
A: Gift wrap.

....

Q: Why did the elf push his bed into the fireplace?
A: Because he wanted to sleep like a log.

Q: What do you get when you cross an apple with a Christmas tree?

A: A pine-apple.

Q: What happened to the monster who ate the Christmas tree?

A: He had to have a tinsel-ectomy.

PETE: Why do you never hear anything about the tenth reindeer, Olive?

JO: Olive?

PETE: You know, "Olive, the other reindeer, used to laugh and call him names."

Q: What do you have in December that you don't have in any other month?

A: The letter D.

Q: Where does Christmas come before Thanksgiving?

A: In the dictionary.

BIRTHDAY JOKES

KNOCK, KNOCK.
Who's there?
Mark.
Mark who?
Mark your calendars—
my birthday is just
around the corner!

Q: What did one candle say to the other?
A: "Don't birthdays burn you up?"

Q: What did the birthday balloon say to the pin?
A: "Hey, Buster!"

Q: What do they serve at birthday parties in heaven?
A: Angel food cake.

Q: What is a geologist's favorite kind of birthday cake?
A: Marble cake.